Creative
BUSINESS
STARTUP

Empowering Creative Women
to Start a Small Business
from Home

Jen Brazeal

Copyright © Jen Brazeal

www.creativebusinessstartup.com

For orders, please email: *info@creativebusinessstartup.com*

ISBN-13: 978-1522863335
ISBN-10:1522863338

Dedication

This book is dedicated to all the women that believe in me as a wife, mom, and business owner. With out your questions I would not have given answers. Also, to my husband, for challenging me to rise to the occasion.

Table of Contents

Chapter One

Welcome to Success

_____

FEAR

You find yourself floundering, waving your arms around, and barely keeping your head above water. Is this really what owning your own business and working from home should be like? Your greatest fear is diving in, saying you can do it, and then closing up shop, not making enough income to support your needs.

Do you have what it takes to succeed and stay in business? Are you unsure of the steps to take to ensure this enterprise can get off the ground?

Creative people are everywhere and really good at what they do, so they take the next step. They turn their skill into a money making business but often do not know how to start or run it effectively. They are good at making and creating, and eventually, along with the skills, the business happens.

Lost and frustrated, they give up. The doors shut, the Etsy shop disappears, and it is over.

They loved taking photographs, making floral bouquets for brides, or teaching sewing classes to groups of kids. But they now realize that there is so much more that goes into owning and RUNNING their own business than they bargained for.

Now it is your turn to give it a go. You have the skill to earn money doing what you love, but the catch is the business side of things: marketing, branding, legalities, and finances. The list goes on and your heart rate quickens; a flustered feeling insides says, "I can't, I don't understand, I don't want to!"

REDEFINE

Stop. Relax. I know exactly how you feel; I have been there, I have started a small business based on my creative talents, and lived to tell about it. Inside this book, you will discover all to the information and tools you need to successfully start and RUN your creative business, all from the comfort of your own home. It is all right here!

The best part is that you are not going to get stressed, feel overwhelmed, or give up. No, you are going to be different. Why? Because you have this book in your hands. You have the steps you need for a creative business startup.

Why is this book what you need? In the early days of my self-employment, I wanted to quit, to go back to how things were before I had to manage money. I dreamed of life before I had to blog every other day and market what I do. I read countless books, spent hours in front of the computer screen, and tried to cut every corner I could. This book cuts all the "fluff" out of starting a business, giving you only exactly what you need.

Why try to figure it out on your own? Why go through the trial and error by yourself? This book will provide some friendly help and guidance, so that you will not want to throw in the towel and walk away.

With each turn of the page, you will start breathing more easily and feel more in control. You are great - amazing actually - at what you create, but the non-creative, business, financial, and legal side of things might be holding you back from realizing your FULL potential. It may be holding you back from quitting your day job, taking a vacation, or simply enjoying your family and life.

I ALWAYS LOVED...

My photography business was born from a simple love of taking pictures. Does that sound familiar? Most small business owners, when asked why they started a business, responded with, "Well I always loved..."

I patiently built a photography company step by step, piece by piece. In my first year, I booked three weddings in three months, and photographed six additional sessions. My second year, I doubled those numbers, while still working full time as an educator, running the business from home in my "free time."

By year four, running my small business turned into the ability to resign from my "day job." I was now a full-time photographer. Even now I continue to grow. As I put new practices and systems in place, I am able to work in my business less and on my business more by applying and using what's written on these pages.

ASSURANCE AND CONFIDENCE

After reading **Creative Business Startup**, you will be more secure with the confidence to say, "I'm a small business owner who succeeds." You will be so confidant in your business, and every facet of how it works, that you will jump at the chance to teach someone else or (dare we say) hire an employee! Hopefully, you will have a profitable and well planned money making machine.

By minimizing frustration, you will be able to bring in more profit while working less. Starting a business is not easy. Throughout these pages, you will become familiar with, and gain vital knowledge on, legally forming your business, marketing your talent, and choosing for whom you want to work. You will gain knowledge about branding your business, using social media, keeping your business in the green, and creating a framework for a business that remains sturdy as it grows and changes.

So cozy up, grab a warm beverage, and get ready to read. You will soon be set up to start your creative business, and gain a few extra pointers to help your business stand out and grow!

STARTUP TOOL KIT

Included with this book is an amazing **Startup Tool Kit**. By using the **Startup Tool Kit's** step-by-step guide and checklist, you can watch your business evolve and track your progress. Charts are included to track productivity and even aid in setting goals.

DO NOT LET ANOTHER DAY SLIP AWAY

Do not read another blog post or google one more LLC or Tax ID question. Do not let another day slip away when you could be bringing in clients, creating a website, and starting up your business the right way, the confusion-free way!

There is no reason to reinvent the wheel, justifying to yourself you can make it on your own. The longer you think, "I can do this on my own, I can figure it out," the more time is lost.

Get ready to start your creative business! These tips, hacks, and quick and easy systems will get you started the right way, with help from famous business entrepreneurs as well as small business owners like yourself. Find the answers to the questions you did not even know you had!

Chapter Two

Branding: It is Not Just a Logo

As a whole, what "makes" your business and sets it apart? Brand your business like a story, making it more of an experience for your clients and customers, rather than a logo. In this chapter new and seasoned business owners will share how they developed their brand and what they learned from others that reduced stress and helped them in their successes.

Before you brand, one thing must be clear: a brand is not a logo. A brand is a feeling or experience you are providing for your client.

At this point, you need to make a few base level decisions; do not think extensively on these, but be sure of what you think. Who are you branding for? Who will be investing in your business? What is your client demographic, what are their interests, where do they shop, and what do they shop for? Are they primarily male or female? What experience will your client have when they invest in your service, and ultimately in your brand.

EXPERIENCING CLASS

For example, consider Chanel. After you pick out that adorable leather handbag, the salesperson certainly does not toss it in a plastic bag that reads "Thank You Thank You Thank You" down the side and say, "Next!" Imagine instead, that it is first placed inside a silk bag for protection, likely monogramed with a large 'C'. Then the handbag is placed in a bed of tissue paper inside a sturdy, clean, classic bag with sturdy handles that will hold up as you stroll down 5th Ave. A black satin ribbon, a flower, or something fancy is affixed for a final embellishment, and a beautiful, finished look.

Chanel, along with many other high end brands, have not only created a quality item for purchase, but they have also provided their clients with an experience that makes them say, "Sure I'll pay $$$$ for that oversized leather bag."

Chanel has created more than a handbag; they created a feeling, an experience that accompanies their product. They instill a sense of affluence, class, and elitism. What will your customers feel when they experience your brand? What will you do to create those feelings?

Think about Lexus; we all recognize their logo as a silver 'L' enclosed in a circle. That logo is so closely associated with their brand. Maybe you have not owned a Lexus but can imagine what it would feel like to take part in their branding experience, fancy leather seats and smooth, quiet rides.

Take Anthropologie for example. What FEELING do you get, or what memories do you have when you think of Anthro? How do those wood floors, inventive décor, and sweet smells make you feel?

Now what do those businesses do to create an experience for the customer, what is their brand all about? Perhaps they selected unique packaging, hired a famous actor to star in their advertisements, chose to communicate in a particular and unique manner, or how they created displays within their stores.

These companies are huge. Small businesses are not nearly that size, hence the name: small business. However, you are still creating, and selling, an experience. Your logo will represent your business and invoke feelings in your customers.

THE CLIENT

Before you pick a name, colors, or fonts, you need to identify who your client is and how you want them to feel about choosing you and your services. What are your clients' goals, income, lifestyle, and hobbies? What makes them happy? Knowing your client before you brand is important because it will help keep you focused. Instead of veering off and creating a brand that you like and you want to buy, you are creating something that they like and want to buy. In some cases, maybe the client is very much like you!

Most clients, however, when you really start to break things down, will not be your twin. Something, or close to everything, may be different. You need to know and understand them so that you can create an experience tailored to their needs and preferences.

Once you identify your intended clientele, stand your ground. In the beginning, while you are building a reputation for a service that caters to a particular type of people. Do not start trying to be everything to everyone. Selling to the masses is not something small businesses can easily do and remain successful long term.

Our natural human impulses tell us to please all those around us. It is difficult to say no in this day and age; in fact, when you are done reading **Creative Business Startup**, I recommend a whole book that touches on the very idea, Boundaries: When to Say Yes, How to Say No to Take Control of Your Life.

Henry Cloud, the author of **Boundaries** said, "Every human being must have boundaries in order to have successful relationships or a successful performance in life." This book centers more on relationships than businesses, but is still very applicable to deciding on your ideal client and sticking with them. We are not right for everyone and everyone is not right for us.

Your level of selectivity when identifying your main client base will be a bold, and perhaps difficult, choice. Can you afford to hold out for your ideal client or do you have a few more bills to pay? If you need to start bringing in money as soon as possible, that is understandable, but do not let that determine your brand. Keep in mind you are still starting your business, and eventually you may grow into being more selective.

This example may help you understand what I mean. If you are a newborn photographer just starting out, do not be afraid to take on a few family photo shoots. It is important to find a balance, being selective, but not so selective that you cannot make any money.

NAMING

Now that you know your ideal client, for whom you are branding, you can more easily pick a name. You will need to choose a name that will serve your business, and therefore your client, appropriately. Will you utilize your own name, or will you come up with a descriptive name? IF you choose to utilize your own name, consider the long term ramifications.

Can it be passed on? Could it be easily sold down the line? On the other hand, if you choose a descriptive name, make it clear. Determine a motto or slogan that accompanies your name.

I knew a couple of girls that wanted to start their own event coordination company. They loved the name Glitter & Glam, but after asking around, they realized that nobody knew exactly what that meant. That was a problem. They decided to add, "tools to plan your event" as their sub-title, their slogan. They included it on their website and on every piece of promotional material, so it became a part of their brand, and pretty much part of their name. They chose to describe what they did while at the same time providing their client with an idea of how Glitter & Glam could help them.

DESCRIPTIVE WORDS

What are three words that describe your brand? If you were telling someone new about your business, how you would introduce yourself in a way that sets you apart? Choose a few words or phrases that describe your style or product that also separate you from your competition. What comes to mind when you close your eyes and picture what you do? Imagine what you want others to see, feel, and perceive when they experience your brand.

There may be a dozen or more words that immediately come to mind. Write all of these down in your "Business Journal." (You have one of those, right?) Out of this word bank, choose the ones that speak to you and elaborate on them. Why did you chose those words and how do they depict your business? Why do you think that those words will draw your client in? How do your words relate to your intended client?

Next time you introduce yourself, instead of a generic, blanket statement such as, "I own a dance studio," add your three words as well as your target client. "Good to meet you too! I own a dance studio that focuses on *young children* with *special* needs. The studio is friendly, secure, and builds confidence."

See how the target market, young children with special needs, was stated and then followed up by your three descriptive words? You have now opened the door to a deeper conversation than if you had just stated that you owned a dance studio. Try to practice this form of introduction the next time you meet a stranger.

CREATING YOUR LOGO

Although a brand is not just a logo, the logo is still an essential component of your brand. Your logo is the stamp you put out there that people will associate with the experience they have at your business. Narrowing down your style and colors can be done in many ways.

One quite simple, but effective, way to determine and develop your logo and brand is Pinterest. Create your board and title it "My Brand." Next, search for the descriptive keywords that describe your brand, those three words you chose just a few minutes ago: modern, light, crisp, crafty, silly, wood, paint, airy, fast. What pops up? Does anything look like it could reflect your business, or does something resonate with your inner creative? Pin it. If it does not reel you in or resonate with you, keep searching. Spend 10 to 12 minutes on this for the next three days. Set your timer on your phone. Do not rush it, but do not skip out either.

You will soon start to see a theme, or even a color palette, emerge on your My Brand board. If you do not see a common theme, ask your spouse or a friend to check it out and provide feedback. While they are checking it, out ask if there is anything that looks out of place or may not go with the flow? You will soon start to see what is not really meshing well with the rest. Remove those pins, as they are not applicable. (Do not feel too badly, Pinterest tends to bring out the scatter brain in the best of us.)

At this point, you have two choices: hire a designer or design your logo yourself.

I started off with designing my logo myself, in Photoshop® using a free font website. Wah wah! It was subpar to say the least but my budget was subpar, so there you go. After about two years, when I had a little money in the bank, I hired a designer that did side jobs. I gave her scattered thoughts on what I wanted and jumped from idea to idea. I was not too sure about who my client was or what I wanted my brand to convey. She ran with my 10 million ideas and created a fun, crafty, cutesy brand, site, and watermark. We went the whole nine yards. I felt official and posted that bad boy all over the place. Things were looking up until I realized that what I had planted all over my work was not a great brand for my business, but rather a great brand for me, Jen. I am crafty and cutesy. I love blues and teals. However, I am not my ideal client. I wanted the clean, classic, and modern bride to look at my brand and my work and say, "Sign me up!" Therefore, I realized that I had to create a logo again and for real this time.

I had a designer in mind from day 1 but she was a professional, and she was expensive. But I knew she would help me along the way and would create a brand that would last years and be timeless like my photography. So although it was a leap, I wrote the check. She was a true New York Designer,and we talked for hours. She forced me to focus, and hone in on my client. She would not accept a vague answer.

Once she had a good feel for who I was, and who my client was, she went to work. Her first round of revisions blew me out of the water. *EVERY SINGLE ONE was perfect. We talked through them and she told me why she did what she did for each one. She was already worth every penny. She even did some mock ups of a new website using the new brands. To me, she was the best designer in the world. One day we are going to sip coffee in Central park and discuss life and such matters.*

I tell you this story for a few important reasons. Even though she was at the top of my budget, your budget may be different than mine. You may need to start off designing your own brand or you may jump right up there and hire a costly design firm. You have to choose where you are. I learned that where I started was not where I finished, and thank goodness.

Hopefully, this story will help you skip some of the heartache, and that what my designer clarified for me, I can clarify for you. Decide correctly now who you are going to serve and know them, own them, and keep them. Decide to design your own logo or hire out.

Creative graphic designer Yuling, of Yuling Designs, shares a little about her personal journey.

"I'm in year four of being my own boss and running my own business. When I first started my business, I was looking around a lot at what was already out there and mimicking what they were doing.

Fast forward a couple of years, I think I have learned a lot more of who I am as a designer, found my own voice, and figured out what I can offer. I'm only now figuring out my own branding and who I want my clientele to be.

I would say that one of the most important things for creating a business brand is evolution! Along the journey of running and growing your own business, you will learn more of who you are and who you want to be as a business. Those things will also evolve along the way. Running a business is an adventure and you have to continually embrace change! Just put yourself out there. You'll continue to learn along the way, and you can continue to rebrand and reinvent yourself as you go."

Yuling hit the nail on the head. Figuring it all out in the first stages may not be a reasonable goal but holding true to where you are now and who your business is is key to keeping your foundation solid. Yes, you will build on your foundation, and it is possible the business five years from now will have grown in a direction you may not have imagined. But that is what evolution is all about!

Shannon, a newborn photographer, provides a great perspective on staying true to your branding adventure.

"I think the most important things I did when creating my brand was to synthesize everything about me and my business down to two big ideas. These were the two things I wanted to be true about my business and true for every client we served. I only wanted two because I wanted them to be memorable, and I wanted them to be measurable. They were and still are: (1) to create beautiful, timeless portraits and (2) to provide personalized and professional customer service. Boom!"

I could not have said it better myself! Simplifying the process of branding can be as easy as choosing two big ideas you want your client to experience and revolving the rest around them.

Great! You should now have a strong feel for branding your business. You heard my personal branding story and realized that I did not have it all figured out straight out of the gate and neither did the Yuling, the graphic designer. You learned more about branding as an experience rather than a logo.

You learned that boundaries in your business and with your clients are essential, and you also chose three words that you plan to use to describe your business. Now it is time to get on to the part of the business side of things that makes you legal. You need to know what finalizes you as a business, not in your own eyes, but in the eyes of ... *the government.*

Do not worry! I am not a lawyer so I am not going to talk like one. This will be one of the easiest but one of the most beneficial chapters when it comes to "officially" starting your business. The goal is for you to understand it and feel secure in your decisions.

Chapter Three

Legalities: Now You Are Looking Official

Get ready to cover some serious ground. Hopefully once this part of starting your business is done, it will only require occasional focus and minimal upkeep. This chapter covers setting up your finances and accounting when forming your business. Do not worry; this is not as scary it sounds.

Just to clarify, I am not a lawyer, and certainly not an accountant. My advice is no substitute for professional counsel. However, I hope to offer you first hand advice, things I learned through my experience and through relationships with other creative small business owners. Once again, just to be clear, this is my personal advice, my opinion or recommendation offered as a guide to action. This chapter should provide you with some base level knowledge on the subject so that when you sit down in your accountant's office, you have a little something in your pocket as far as vocabulary and familiarity on the subject goes.

I have learned so much through trial and error, spending hour upon hour in front of the computer searching for answers. When in doubt, I asked a professional, and encourage you to do the same. Once I thought I knew what was good for me and my business, I went to a trusted professional and double checked. Ultimately, I hired a lawyer and paid to have them help me set up my business correctly and legally.

EIN

An Employer Identification Number is similar to a social security number but for your business. It separates you from your work. At least for me, keeping business as separate as possible, both financially and legally, is for the best. If Al Pacino and Meg Ryan have taught us anything in their on-screen roles, it would be that "It's not personal, it's strictly business." If you plan on buying from a wholesaler or opening a business bank account (which you will), then you will need an EIN. To obtain this, apply for one with the IRS.

BUSINESS BANK ACCOUNT

Opening a business bank account is a huge step towards having an official business. Not only does it make you *feel* official, but you actually are official.

Here is what it will look like to open your "big girl" account. You will use your EIN number and walk (maybe strut a little) through those doors, ask (in a very mature way) to speak to someone about opening a business bank account, then you will hand over your first check for deposit. (Okay, this check may be $52.78 but it was hard earned.)

First I would urge you to select a bank in your area. I emphasize this local aspect of selecting a bank, because I found that larger and national banks charge fees for business accounts. Often, a personal checking account is free and advertised all over the place, but a business account you pay for.

When I started looking at a few, smaller local banks, I found that a lot of them offered free business banking. Jackpot! Not only were they local, so I could go in and bombard them with a million questions, but they gave me their personal emails and phone numbers. So far, I have not ever had to wait on hold or had to press 1, then 7, then 4, then yell "operator" into the phone, simply to have the service revert back to the starting menu.

My banker answers the phone and he answers my emails the same day, often within the hour. While this is not typical, and may not be the case for you, going local was perfect for me. We set up accounts and set limits to help prevent fraud all for the cost of sitting in my banker's office (that means it was free).

I perform all my business transactions from this account, and it is linked to my accounting software. Handling the accounting this way keeps my life organized and my business completely separate from my personal life.

INSURANCE

After you have obtain your EIN and set up your business bank account, then it is time to shop for business insurance.. While you hope to never have to use it, having it will provide piece of mind at least, and recovery from losses at best. While you may think you are too small or that a small mishap will not affect you, once you start getting a paycheck from your business or hire employees, Murphy's Law will be in full effect. Somewhere along the way, mistakes happen and having insurance helps to keep the business running during those times, instead of coming to a halt.

I selected a larger insurance company that had a specific plan for what I do, photography. They were able to explain to me all I needed to get covered, and they charge me a one-time yearly payment. I still have mixed emotions about paying for this, since chances are I will never even use it once, While it is a large business expense, it also ensures I will never face a major setback financially.

MYTH BUSTED

I do not need a business bank account; I will just be very careful with my personal account.

For legitimacy and legal reasons, you do need a business account. As you read about above, to keep any legal matters contained to your business, and not affecting your personal finances, you need to show a separate business account. It is also pertinent for paying taxes appropriately and staying fiscally organized. Besides any IRS auditing issues that may arise over the years, you will also feel and appear much more professional when dealing with clients' money.

I do not need insurance; I am a very small business, so it is just not relevant.

Once I brought on associates, business insurance was required, and the list grew of all the possible scenarios that could take place once I was not the only one involved in my business. You may be related, or very close, to the people you bring on. While we do not want to believe that a problem or accident would be blamed on us as owners, it can easily happen. Do not expose yourself or your business in this manner. Get insured and reduce vulnerability. BONUS: it is generally accepted as a tax deduction!

Take Action

In your preferred browser, use the search terms: small business insurance. While the search will result in many options, scroll through and select three. Of these three, thoroughly investigate their website, to determine if they may suit your needs.

If none of your initial selections fit your needs, choose another three, or streamline your search by adding the type of creative business you are in to the search terms, such as: small business insurance voice lessons.

Once you find a company that seems well suited to your needs, email or call to set up a time to talk about what you need. At the very least, general liability insurance is coverage that can protect you from a variety of claims including bodily injury, property damage, personal injury, and other scenarios that can arise from your business operations.

MYTH BUSTED

I cannot pay myself, I barely have enough money in my account as it is.

If you are not paying yourself, then what is the fun in having your own business? If you still have a full time job, then your creative startup may still be a hobby. But if this is your full time job, and you are putting in full time hours, then you should be paying yourself.

You own this business, so you can make an owner's draw whenever you want. Start off by paying yourself monthly. Yes, you will have to do a little math to make sure that you do not go in the red, and the first paychecks may be less than what you hope for long term, but this is going to build your confidence, make you feel like you are contributing to household finances, and give you a little something to live on!

BUSINESS FORMATION

Whoa! You made it through those first three things. Hopefully they were less scary than they seemed in the beginning, and they are necessary to setting up a legitimate business. Next, you will need to choose a legal status for your business. Unfortunately, it will require more thought and effort than the "it's complicated" type of status. While I am not an accountant or lawyer, I will provide you with the creative's take on the three different ways to file your business: Sole Proprietorship, LLC or S-Corp.

Sole Proprietor

A Sole Proprietor is pretty much what it sounds like: one person doing business. You will more than likely also file a DBA, Doing Business As, along with your Sole Proprietorship, and your business taxes will be included on your personal taxes, like self-employment.

Even though becoming a Sole Proprietor sounds easy, it can be a drain on your time. From my conversations with fellow business owners, this seems like the best option when starting out, but most will shift away from this early in their business, within the first two years. This type of filing is the most closely related to your personal finances and taxes, and to the world, and therefore your clients, there will not be much of a distinction.

LLC

An LLC is a Limited Liability Company (or Corporation). I know, this is starting to sound so fancy! For the most part, a lot of what you do for a Sole Proprietor will be the same that you do for an LLC, with one tiny difference. That difference may be small, but it can have a HUGE impact: your business assets are the *only* thing that can be touched in a legal situation. Once again, like the insurance policy, this just adds an additional layer of protection for all the what-ifs associated with your business.

If you plan to have a partner, opening an LLC is a solid option, as there are different filings you can set up to distribute profit. Some states do require an additional tax for an LLC, so make sure to check the IRS website for the specifics in your state.

S-Corp

Last, but not least, is an S-Corp. An S-Corp is more complicated because it includes incorporating shareholders into your company and profits. If you are the only business person it is possible to set yourself up as the single shareholder. You are also required to be paid a salary, at least at the rate of an equivalent job in the general marketplace.

Take Action

If one of these sounded like a good fit, dive deeper. Research what your state may require for the filing you are interested in. As the owner of a creative small business, you will most likely be sticking with the Sole Proprietorship or LLC, so go ahead and get your professional tax or legal consultant to help you pull the trigger and set this up.

ACCOUNTING

You are now ready for the fun part: accounting! I may be the least accountant-like person you will ever meet, but as soon as I got the correct system in place, accounting became just another step in my business.

Accounting allows you to see and track your business progress, stay ahead of the game when it comes time to pay yearly, quarterly, or monthly taxes, and to pull data or run reports that reflect the health of your business.

I started my business on spreadsheets. At first, I had about 20 of them, and my system worked fine; money came in and went out, mileage was logged, and equipment tracked. Then, I added employee spreadsheets, itemized expenses, office and rent expenses, more equipment, and the list kept growing and growing. I started getting confused on what I should be naming all of these spreadsheets, much less keeping up with them! Not only that, with each new year, I had to start all over.

I was spending so much time on this that it was difficult to determine where my business was financially. I knew from my bank account that I was at least in the green, but for how long? Spreadsheets and a limited Quickbooks® knowledge did not a business make..

I quickly, and thankfully, handed all my sheets over to my accountant and said good luck, after which I assumed she probably banged her head against the desk or had a good cry. After she probably collected herself and gathered the strength to dial my number, she called me back for clarifications. She did not know who or what all my charges were for on my spreadsheets, and I had to go back and remember from months ago what I purchased, why I did it, or who needed it. This took hours of backtracking, finding receipts, and trying to decode my bank account. It took a lot of time, and a lot of my accountant's billed time.

While Quickbooks® is an excellent tool, it is not perfect for everyone. In fact, your small creative business may not need all it has to offer. I knew it was a powerful tool, but I was so busy organizing my spreadsheets, that I never took the time to learn it. I know--- the irony!

There are dozens of online accounting services that link to your bank account and do only what you need them to do. They track your expenses and income and categorize it, simply and easily. If you are a small business (to me that means 5 or less are involved financially with your business) like myself, you may need a simplified version of accounting software.

Take Action

Here are a few online services to get you started. Compare, but they all cover the basics. Just pick one!

www.godaddy.com/email/online-bookkeeping

www.waveapps.com

www.lessaccounting.com

www.xero.com/us/accounting-software

www.freshbooks.com/right-for-me

There are so many more and no, I did not receive any kickbacks for listing these. They are just good accounting programs I have come across that you can use online, on any device. Check one out and sign up. You will soon be on your way to tracking and predicting your business finances. It can actually feel fun and can get you more excited about what you do!

Julie, a long time accountant, has a little bit of encouragement before discussing taxes next.

"One of the most important things you can do when starting a business is to find a good CPA to help you navigate your finances and tax responsibilities. Find someone who is easy for you to talk to and can help you understand the financial and tax aspects of your business. Your accountant can help you set up a system of accounting and reporting that will guide you on your path to success in your new venture. Your financial reports tell the story of your business. Let your accountant help you make it a story of success!"

TAXES

Last, but most certainly not least, are your business taxes. I actually cried the first time I tried to file my business taxes on my own (yes, tears were streaming).

Like most of your creative startups, my business began in my home.

My husband and I had recently moved in the same calendar year, I had made some purchases for my business, opened accounts, and made other transactions. I had to calculate square footage from both homes, expenses utilities, and create a schedule of my equipment. I also had no idea what a schedule of equipment even was.

My husband looked at me and said, "Hire someone." Notice that his sentence ended with a period. He wanted me to stop crying and fix the problem. For my sanity, and also his, he did not want to join me in analyzing my business from every direction.

He was confident that I knew the solution, and I did. I wanted to save money by doing it on my own, or at least cajoling him into doing it for me. But when all is said and done, hiring an outside source to get me on track and set me up for the future was the best decision yet.

The first year that I filed as a real business and hit the books, I realized that I barely had enough dough to cover the taxes my business had incurred. Yes, I had been collecting sales tax but I was not managing it appropriately. At the beginning of your business, like mine, you may not be making enough money to file quarterly or monthly taxes. You will pay once annually. I was ill equipped for this, to say the least.

To avoid ever being caught off guard when tax time comes, because it *will* come in the United States of America, start now, setting aside 25 to 30 percent of every dollar you bring in. Place it in a separate account, but attached to your business account, perhaps marked as savings. Do not touch it except for paying taxes.

This may seem like a lot of money to set aside if you are used to traditional employment, where this is typically done automatically for you. The difference here is that you see it, you know it is there, and that kind of makes it harder to take away.

MYTH BUSTED

This is just a hobby, so I do not worry about taxes.

If you do not charge a single dime for your services or products and you have $0 profit, then you are correct. However, the moment you receive monetary payment for your skills, service, or product, you will owe taxes.

We covered serious ground in this chapter. We discussed EINs, bank accounts, and business insurance. You even got to check out some great websites so that you can start keeping your books the accurate and painless way. Tips like setting aside money for taxes and some light definitions on forming your business were pretty uncomplicated. That was not as painful as you thought, right?

There is no need to avoid any of these aspects of your business now that you have a more clear understanding of them. Make sure to check them off the **Business Startup Checklist** in the back of the book.

In the next chapter, I will discuss the true meat and potatoes of setting up your business. It can seem arduous and maybe even a little futile to do so much planning, and most creative entrepreneurs want to skip over this to just start selling and making money. But you are different, you want to be as successful as possible, and you are reading *this* book. Creating a framework in your business will help it prosper and will set you apart from your competition. Building a framework that is strong and will last helps ensure that your business will flourish.

Chapter Four

Framework: Setting Up For Success

Some skip over this next step is getting your business up and running; many dislike it though due to lack of understanding. DO NOT be like the others! As you dive deeper into the framework of your business, you will learn how to set up and structure the inner workings of your business through systems, prototypes, and more. You will also read about a multi-million dollar company starting from the ground and rising up, up, up!

Prominent financial guru, Dave Ramsey says, "People are in such a hurry to launch their product or business that they seldom look at marketing [and business] from a bird's eye view, and they don't create a systematic plan."

WHO IS THE HERO?

This next section is inspired by an amazing company called Storyline. Please check them out if what you read resonates or makes you think, "ah, of course!" For me, it changed everything. Hopefully it can also make a difference for you!

It is typical human behavior to feel that others want to know your story. But really, they feel the same way, and want you to know about them.

To potential customers, your business is not about you. It is not about who did it or how the business got started; it is not about the journey you have taken to get to where you are. Although those things are important, and a huge part of your business, they are mainly important to you, not to your client.

For your client, you are a solution to their problem, a fulfillment for their need. In your own life story, you are hopefully the hero, the main character. You travel through your life, your story, looking for solutions to your problems, looking for a guide. The guide for others can be you and your business!

Start considering your client as the star of their story. They are looking for someone to help solve their problem, and that is you. You are not the hero, *they* are.

Putting this idea out there on your website, social media, and in your conversations about business will change the way you do things. You are now the problem solver, the guide to someone else's story. To become the master, you must first learn to serve.

Let this simple realization be the first block in building your framework foundation.

THE FOUR TENETS OF A SOLID FOUNDATION

While this section covers a lot of ground, it is pretty even ground; there are no huge uphill battles here. For me, this is the bread of butter of self-employment, the part that I have really grown to enjoy about running my own business. The keyword here is "grown," as I have not always felt this way.

I want to help you regain your sanity, have some much needed time away from work, and get a good night's sleep, all while still running a successful business. If you are someone who often stays awake at night, staring at the ceiling, with thoughts in your head, this part is for YOU!

These four tenets of a solid foundation are the building blocks for a sturdy structure, one that stands the test of time. It is worth mentioning again that where I am in my business is largely in part to what I have learned from countless books, blogs, workshops, and experiences. I have modified all of these to work for my unique business. A huge help and a fairly quick and easy read is ***The E-Myth Revisited: Why Most Small Businesses Don't Work and What to Do About It*** by Michael E. Gerber. The *E-Myth* gives you an overall

_____

picture of the infrastructure of business big and small. Like the quote from Dave Ramsey above, it is a bird's eye view.

① Three Roles

At some point, your skills prompted others to desire your service, asking "how much?" You decided to start a business and here you are. While this may be new information, you now have a triply split personality! You are the entrepreneur, technician, and manager of your company!

Entrepreneur- This role involves coming up with ideas, providing motivation, and encouraging innovation.

Technician- This role revolves around the skills needed to keep a business afloat, and the know-how of doing so. In a creative start up, this is the role many of us find ourselves in the most often, making, creating, and doing! The technician is the "talent," so to speak.

Manager- This is the role that requires organization, and the ability to implement elements of production. This person makes sure that things get done, in a timely manner and with the expected quality.

All of these are the roles needed for a small business to function. Early on in your small business, you will have to be all three roles, hence the split personality. In the long run, you may choose others to fulfill these roles, hiring managers, researchers, etc. For now, get comfortable with wearing all of those hats, and wearing them well. If you can do this, you will already be off to a great start!

This start however, requires time, time, and more time, so do not be discouraged with the tedious business of getting things up and running!

2 **Prototype**

Think of any successful franchise. Because they make the world's best frozen lemonade, Chick-Fil-A comes to my mind pretty easily. (On a side note, if you have not had one, try it. Your life will be changed!) In the beginning there was one Chick-Fil-A, and eventually they multiplied, with replicas following due to demand.

Think about ordering their chicken sandwich or any experience at their counter. What does a Chick-Fil-A employee say to you after you say, "thanks?" Is it the same thing every time, is it not? No matter what state you are in, or what time you order it, the response is the same. How does that happen? Despite differences in employees and geography, each experience remains similar, meeting expected standards.

This is a natural result of the franchise model. Build and run your business as if you were going to make 1000 just like it and you are the first *one*. What do you need to do to make sure everything runs like clockwork and smoothly? While most of us will not ever need to replicate our business having this mind set will ensure a clean and organized "first one".

 Systems, Systems, and More Systems

> *"A system is a set of things, actions, ideas,*
> *and information that interact with each other, and in*
> *so doing, alter other systems."*

> \- Michael E. Gerber

When I first began considering the systems I needed to put in place at my business, I knew they would need refinement, that I needed to be detailed and specific. I needed to know what I expected out of my business, and employees, forwards and backwards. I had to have them down to an art! I needed to build my systems as if I was leaving my whole business unattended, the business that I had worked years to create. The systems I put in place would allow for me to leave my steady income, and my future security, in the hands of someone else.

I was going on maternity leave. I was taking 12 whole weeks completely off.

When I first began my business, I was single. Fast forward a few years, and my husband and I were hearing a tiny heartbeat in a doctor's office. Right then I knew that things were about to get crazy, in my personal life, yes, but also for my business. I am sure that some of you can relate! I am not the only one, right?

I wanted to have it all; I wanted to go on maternity leave, and I needed my business to work even when I was not there. I took 12 weeks completely off. I may have snuck in to my email account a few times to check my inbox, but that was about it. There was no product fulfillment, newsletter writing, or social media post completed on my own time; I was on vacation for 12 weeks, or at least off of work; I do not think that staying home with a newborn could really be described as a vacation!

But how did I stay away and still manage to book six new clients, manage current customers, and continue to get paid during that time?

I started considering the small things. I mused over my simple day-to-day routine: sitting at the computer, posting to Instagram, answering emails for 15 minutes, writing a blog post, taking a coffee break, picking photos and stories for the next newsletter, sending welcome gifts to new clients, and ordering Christmas gifts for previous clients.

I began listing out all of the things I did on a daily basis. Then I created a list of everything that I wanted to get done over the next few weeks, and the next few months, and began tackling them in that order. I started with the small and simple things and went from there

Identifying the systems you need to have in place for your business to function allows you to perfect the steps it takes to achieve your desired outcome. Systems let you hand off parts of your business to others. In return for this clarity and direction, employees (or future employees) can work in your business, while you work on it. (Or in the case of maternity leave, I could work on keeping a tiny, new, infant alive!)

With systems identified and in place, you get to do the fun stuff, the stuff you thought you would be doing far more of when you first had that "ah-ha" moment and thought, "I can go into business for myself!" Creating systems for things you wish that you did not have to do, things you love, and things you did not even realize that you did, will provide you with a fresh perspective on your business!

4 Manuals

Along with a system comes the ability, and need, to create a manual. When I first started my business, I created short documents that were basically steps listed in bullet point format, with added detail below each. I did this long before I ever even dreamed that I would want, or need, to hire someone to come on board with me.

What is a manual? A manual is simply a system written in a manner that others can understand and carry out. Since I used to be a teacher, I thought of my manuals as plans for a substitute teacher. I created a plan for my typical day, what needed to be completed and when, what tools were needed, and how to get each step done. Is it any surprise that during my teaching career, I was known for doing an insanely thorough job creating these? Even in my absence, my classroom had routines, systems, and policies to keep it running quite smoothly. I did not want my lack of presence to create chaos.

My plans for a roomful of first graders were usually around eight pages, color coded, and included picture symbols. Those plans were just for the morning, before lunch! As you can imagine, this level of specificity was not written out for the substitute in a single sitting. I thought through all the questions that could come up, all the scenarios that needed to be covered. It took time.

The time I spent helped ensure that what needed to get done did indeed get done, and in the manner to which my students were accustomed, to the level of quality and thoroughness that I expected.

Right now, creating a manual may seem ridiculous. You know what needs to get done, how to do it, and you are the only one around! But if your business becomes successful, and I hope that it does, it will grow, and you will not be able to do everything on your own. At some point, you may need additional help to complete online orders, answer additional emails, receive and make payments, open a storefront, or answer phones.

After you hire your first employee, you cannot just simply say "help me" and expect them to jump right in. This employee will be expected to do things like you do them, and instead of trying to write it all down in the thick of things, writing it all down now will help you train your employee quickly and efficiently, at the time that you need them!

MYTH BUSTED

I will write my manuals when I need to hire someone, but right now I am too busy.

Do you think that when you hire someone to help you out, because you are completely overwhelmed, that you will suddenly have more time to do these more tedious tasks? When I made myself start writing manuals for each system, I took it one task at a time, opening a blank document and immediately diving into steps and bulleted lists. I quickly found my groove and had over 23 tasks in my manual within an hour! In order to "test" your manual, hire a friend, neighbor, or even your babysitter to come over and see if they can follow your steps. You could even sweeten the deal by offering to pay them $10 or giving them a gift card for helping you out. If the manual passes the test, then that means that someone you hire could follow your directions and get something done in your business, while you enjoy other aspects or even life outside of work, such a cooking or running errands!

BUILD IT IN FROM THE BEGINNING

This is your chance to build your brand even more. By using your systems to add small, consistent, well-thought out details into each client interaction, your clients begin to actually experience your brand.

You may have grand intentions of sending a personalized note card saying thank you for an order, or for booking your services, but without a system in place to ensure completion of this task, it *will* fall through the cracks. When you build marketing and branding into your systems from the beginning, you ensure that your business runs smoothly in the manner you prefer, with the same result every time!

This does not give you an excuse to put your innovative mind set on the shelf. Your systems and manual will need to be updated as you simplify, grow, research, and find ways to increase productivity. Once manuals are made they are not set in stone. But modifying a previously made manual is much less time consuming that creating one from scratch, especially if you update on a consistent basis, or at least when changes to procedures are made.

Setting up detailed systems is another way to set yourself apart from other creative businesses just starting up. The customer experience will be consistent and your product reliable. This reputation will go far!

OUTSOURCE

Outsourcing can be oh-so-beautiful. (Do you hear angels singing somewhere right now?) I will actually go out on a limb and guarantee that once you outsource something that is consuming the majority of your time on a daily basis, you will not regret it.

Think about something many people do to free up time: hiring a cleaning service. Assuming that someone can afford this and that the service does a good job, who is really going to sit around thinking, "Man, I really wish I was on my hands and knees scrubbing when I could have been fixing dinner, relaxing after the kids were asleep, or working on my business?" More commonly, the response would be, "Wow! What a relief to hire this service to come take care of something I could do, but that is taking my valuable time and attention away from more important and productive things."

Outsourcing is the same concept. Yes, you could do it yourself and save a few dollars now, but should you? Would your business be better served if you were working on things that were evolving and developing your business, things that *only* you could do? Only you can make personal visits or phone calls, but is your presence necessary when licking stamps and mailing packages? Spending a little to take care of a lot, all while producing more, is always a great idea!

Obviously, outsourcing may not be the first thing you do when starting your business, but it may come more quickly than you thought. So not wait and put off something that someone else could be doing for you, freeing you up for more valuable things. Hand over your manual and move on.

While this chapter covered the foundations for creating the framework of your business, as well as additional considerations, setting up the framework is time-consuming and needs to be well-planned.

Fulfilling the three main roles your company needs to thrive, determining a prototype, identifying systems, and writing manuals will set your business apart from other creative startups. Building the framework from the beginning, and outsourcing as needed, will save valuable time (and therefore cost) down the road!

Always remember that the sooner you act on a need, or a potential need, the better. Your mind is the most valuable resource in your business. Stay organized, using systems to free you up to make improvements and decisions. Remember, the client needs to feel like the hero of the story, and to create this experience, things need to run smoothly. Your focus needs to be on them, and not on everything else that should have been done from the beginning.

As your business starts to stabilize you will want to channel the greatness of your business into a very useful tool: a website. Developing your presence online and establishing your brand in the social media realm is what opens your (figurative) doors to the public.

Chapter Five

Social Media + Website: Virtual Storefronts

This is probably the chapter you have been waiting for, where the fun really begins! Chapter five covers social media and your business website.

This part of the business has been overwhelming for me; I feel like I can never keep up. While you may feel the same way, remember that so far, you have been organized, and you prepared (you are reading this, after all)! As your business unfolds and becomes more public, a website or social media account can help you connect to customers, develop your brand, and advertise your services or goods.

There is a reason this chapter did not come first. While it can be exciting, or even fun, you first need to build a strong foundation. Slow and steady wins the race, right? Do you want to be the tortoise or the hare? However, at this point in your race, it is time to build an online marketplace. Your presence on the internet can be the largest and most important aspect of your marketing campaign, if done correctly.

This chapter could be its own book. In fact, many books have been written on this topic. However, I intend to keep it basic, as this is the start of your creative business. Over time, you can investigate ways to grow and expand your online presence, using the internet to your advantage.

YOUR WEBSITE

Donald Miller, of Storyline Blog, which was mentioned earlier in Chapter Four, is an author, movie writer, speaker, and so much more. He helps businesses build their brands through telling a story. He has already taught that in your business, you are not the hero, but rather your client is. Your business is all about the client, and your job is to guide them or provide a solution. Like your brand and systems, your website should be all about the hero, the client. Making your website all about you and your company, leaving the hero or key player out of the mix, is a recipe for disaster.

Designer versus Do It Yourself

Designing a website, much like designing your logo, can be done in one of two ways: hiring out or doing it yourself. So much of starting a business is dependent on you and your desired lifestyle and budget.

Think about where you are right now. More than likely, you are just starting out, creating this business from your living room or home. While you may have little space or resources to work with, you know that whatever needs to be done should be completed efficiently and accurately.

If you are hiring a website designer, choose someone that you trust, but also *knows* your particular industry. A great designer will guide you along the way and walk you through each decision that must be made, Hiring a web designer means that you do not have to have all the answers..

If you cannot hire a designer for this step (or simply do not wish to), keep in mind that your website is a very big deal. It is your virtual storefront, the customer's first impression of your business. In many cases, your clients may be interacting with your site for more time than they interact with you. With photography for example, they may be looking at albums, ordering prints, booking a session, and so much more! The website needs to be easy to use, direct, and informative. Your client should be able to spend minimal time on your website and get a sense of security, that you are the right person for their job.

Take Action

Decide right now if you plan to design your website on your own or hire a designer. Yes, now. If you feel strongly about hiring someone, ask your peers and colleagues in your field for recommendations. Search sites, and when you come across one that you love, send the business a message and ask who designed it. If you decide to go with your own site or blog, find a provider for this purpose, such as Wordpress.com, register your URL or domain name, open an account that suits your needs, and choose a template!

SEO: The Tip of the Iceberg

When choosing your URL or domain name, think about the big picture, the way it will be searched for and used, and if it will stand the test of time. Is it easy to find online? Try searching for it yourself, or ask a friend to do it. Is it too long, giving people too many opportunities for errors? Does it make sense? Is it simple and direct? Since you will most likely be paying an annual fee to "rent" the URL (or possibly spending bigger money to own it), then make sure that it will be applicable to your business long term, despite growth and change.

Keeping and developing your URL long term is important for 2 major reasons. First, building your site with included keywords and permalinks will allow for Search Engine Optimization (SEO). When potential clients Google you or your business, it helps maintain a better position in the ranked results list. Secondly, if you change your address, even an online address, it will cause confusion, and people may not be able to find you. Think of it the same way as if you moved four times in a year. Will all of your friends follow up to find the current one come the holidays, or will you be left off of the Christmas card list? Make sure people can find you, quickly and easily

Wordpress, as I mentioned above, is a platform used to design your own site. They even have a convenient plug-in you can download that walks you through some SEO "must dos." If you do not love any of the templates offered with your subscription, others can be purchased for a minimal amount, and are fairly easy to install.

Including a weblog, or blog for short, as part of your site is great for your SEO. This format provides the opportunity to expand on products and gives clients the chance to connect with you in a variety of ways. If you are using a blog to maximize your online potential, keep a few things in mind:

1. Stay consistent on blog posts.
2. Keep your content relevant and meaningful to your business.
3. Match keywords and permalinks to increase your SEO.
4. Include photos (and rename those photos to support your keywords).
5. Check yo gramma!

Site Simplicity

Within a single glance, your client should understand what it is you sell, no matter if it is a product or service. Make what you are offering obvious to your client. Test this out on friends or family if need be.

Then take it one step further; make it even easier to contact you! This is your personal business, so be truthful and up front about who you are, what you do, and what can be expected when interacting with you. For instance, let your client know the best times to reach you, the best way to get a hold of you, and the average turnaround time for your response to an inquiry.

When it comes to your craft, your knowledge scale of the product or service is most likely at least a nine on a scale of one through ten. However, your average client is probably shopping around with a knowledge level of somewhere around a two. Remember that what is obvious to you is not always obvious to potential clients. Stay simple, straightforward, and informative. Tell them what the service or product that you provide is as if you were talking in bullet points:

- I design high-end birthday invitations.
- We make motivational signs.
- I photograph your wedding.
- Our company plans events.
- I teach sewing lessons after school.

Do not get too fancy at first. Make your craft clear, so that interested clients stay on your post, bookmark, or remember the site. Make it easy and simple for clients to know right off the bat that you can fix their problem with your business. On deeper levels of your site, you can always provide more details.

Site Navigation

Easy navigation throughout, ability to find pricing, and an online store are all key components to effective site navigation. Making a potential client go on a scavenger hunt for information is an easy way to lose them!

If your services or products are customized, and price is determined on a case-by-case basis, provide viewers with averages. Be as honest as possible. You can even mention different circumstances that may raise or lower the price such as, "An average wedding invitation design is $$$. However, if you want something special and unique, our personal design packages start at $$$$."

Let your client know what to expect. Nothing is worse than finding out you are in the wrong packed movie theater after it has begun. Do not get caught having to say "excuse me, sorry, pardon me, excuse me, so sorry," as you step on all those feet.

This is your first time to build trust with your client. If the prices you list scare them off, then they were not your client to begin with. I know booking a client or selling a product is so important right now, especially in the beginning, but do not compromise for it. An amazing man and wonderful speaker, Zig Ziglar, once said, *"Be careful not to compromise what you want most for what you want now."*

In designing a website, here is a loose structure to start you off. Including these five sections in your site will provide clarity and give you a place to start.

1. INTRO PAGE - Include your customer's wants or needs.
2. INTRO PAGE - Point out the problems your client may have.
3. WORK WITH ME PAGE - What can you say to let your client know you understand what they are going through?
4. ABOUT PAGE - What can you do or offer that makes you the best choice?
5. CONTACT PAGE - Call them to act.

SOCIAL MEDIA

Now that you have your website up and running, it is time to set up social media accounts. Since this is a business startup, the goal is to keep this simple and cover the basics. Utilizing social media for the benefit of your business is a huge step; it is your social voice and style, and it puts your brand out there for the world to experience. A personal or more intimate post can provide potential clients with a snapshot of what they will experience if they hire you!

At this point, depending on your service or products, you must decide if you will be utilizing your personal accounts, making them work for your business, or if you will be creating separate business accounts.

How involved do you want your clients to be in your personal life? Do you use your current private account for business, or mainly for updating friends and family on your life? If you currently use social media to post daily pictures of your dog or toddler, are you willing to give that up in order to appear more professional? In some cases, you may be answering these questions in a positive manner. If so, then perhaps using your existing personal accounts is right for you.

However, if you prefer to remain business focused on your business accounts, and keep them separate from your personal life, then you should probably open new accounts for that purpose. While you can include parts of your personal online presence, think about what proportion of your posts should be strictly business versus personality? Is 80/20 a good ratio for you? 60/40?

Try to determine this on the front end and stick to it.

If you are unsure, browse various companies on different social media platforms. What ratio does it seem like they use? Do they get personal? If so, is that something that connects you or makes you unsure if you want to do business with them. Think about what your ideal client may think or feel.

MYTHS BUSTED

My personal Facebook page can also be my business page, I do not think I can manage two.

Facebook has many rules and formulas for effectiveness and use. Facebook actually discourages using your personal page as your business page as well, but rather provides opportunity for two separate accounts, though linked. If they feel that you are violating their rules, they can and will shut down your page (either personal or business) anytime they feel like it. Remember that you do not actually own your Facebook page, Facebook does. If they feel that you are using a particular type of account outside their limits and rules, then they can shut it down.

I am too busy for social media right now.

We are in an era of digital advertisements, electronic communication, and even online education; having an online presence is crucial. There are even ways to post to social media while away from your computer – you are no longer tied to a physical office or desk.

There are also platforms out there that are free and will post when you want, where you want, and what you want. Hootsuite, for example, is a program that allows users to write posts ahead and time, then will post to your Facebook, Instagram, LinkedIn, Google+, or Twitter accounts at specified times in the future, so that you can enjoy life knowing the posting is handled. This does not mean that the days of sitting down and posting on your own are gone. It just means that there are tools out there to help you be more engaged more frequently.

I need more likes/followers to be successful.

Sometimes it feels like our society is still back in high school, trying to navigate the popularity contest. Social media can feel like that at times. Keep in mind that more likes are not always better likes. Quality is better than quantity. It is easy to think these thoughts, but it is much harder to really believe them? If you are bringing in clients, and making a profit too, then it really does not matter if you have four likes or 4,000.

Organic growth takes time, and you want people to like your pages and posts that are truly engaged and interested in your products or services. Otherwise, the numbers mean nothing. It is better to have a few that love you than many that just like you. (I also believe that this is true outside of business as well).

I found an app that will get me 10,000 followers in 2 days!

Beware of anyone, ever, that promotes overnight success. Remember: quality over quantity. This goes back to what your business needs to be successful. Does it need 10,000 likes from uninterested strangers? Probably not, as they will not bring anything to the business table.

I have been looking at the Instagram account belonging to one of my competitors. They seem so successful; should I try to do what they are doing?

I will not be the first to utter this phrase, but I started saying it to my husband a while back when we were going through a lot of personal and financial changes, all in the midst of moving to a new town. "Comparison is the root of all evil." This may sound a bit drastic, I know, but it certainly would make us stop and really think.

Every situation, business, person, and client is different. Consider unfollowing that person that is, "doing so well." You are not learning how to run *your* business better by pining over their posts comments. There are enough hurdles for you to jump over as you start a business, without comparing yourself via social media.

Your competitor has different goals and a different version of success than you do. Keep thinking "Apples and oranges, apples and oranges!"

I have not ever really been a huge fan of sharing my personal life. I was not extremely active on social media anyways, so to combine some personal posts with business ones was easier for me than to try and separate them out. If you are active online and on social media, and you love sharing your personal images, thoughts, and stories, then perhaps you need to have a separate business focused account where you splash personal in every once in a while. You can curate these posts to fit your brand, but still reflect the real "you." This is your decision; look at your own brand, your own life (the personal side and business side), and make the decision that is right for you, right now.

Chapter Six

Marketing:
The Meat of Your Business

"I'm just not a salesperson; I cannot sell things." Does that sound familiar?

That is right, it is time to talk about marketing. WAIT! Do not close the book. Jumping into an area that feels unnatural or that you have no clue about can be intimidating. There is no reason to throw in the towel now, and I will do my best to help you through this next step little by little. You will be prepared and you will do great!

While billboards, commercials, and print advertisements are options for big businesses, you are just beginning, and most likely do not have the money in the bank to plan such a large marketing campaign. You just filed your DBA and purchased insurance. You may have outsourced some website design or hired someone to carry out a system using a manual. So you do not have the funds to purchase a national ad (or a need for that matter).

MARKETING YOURSELF

You are the biggest advocate for your brand, so make sure your mindset in terms of marketing revolves around this fact. If you are not excited about your business, or sharing that excitement, then who will? In a small business startup, you will likely be the entire marketing department, along with most other departments. Everything you do, from returning phones calls on time to promptly answering emails, is part of your marketing strategy. Perhaps you want to ship orders with a cute ribbon and handwritten note. Yes, that is marketing too.

Everything you do, every feeling you invoke and experience you provide, is part of your brand and serves as marketing for your business. You are a walking billboard for your own business, advertising yourself at professional networking events and also while checking out in the grocery line.

How is it possible to promote yourself without feeling like you are pushing a sale? Get comfortable with and *practice* a new way of introductions. This introduction is less of a sales pitch and more of a way to help someone else solve a problem.

Perhaps you are at the grocery store one day and you are interacting with Sally, the cashier:

" **You:** "Hi, how's your day going?"

Sally: "Fine."

You: "Those are nice earrings on, where did you get them?"

Sally: "What, these old things? I don't even remember."

You: "They're so cute. I noticed them since I actually make earrings. I'd love to give you a fresh new pair, just for fun?

Sally: "Really?"

You: "Yes! Here's my card. Visit my site online and pick a pair you love. Just email me, and I'll bring them by next time I need milk!"

Yes, you gave away a pair of earrings but consider the long term effect. Sally is going to tell everyone she knows that she was just scanning food at work and you came by with a sweet unexpected gift, just for her!

Think back on our discussion for putting systems in place from the very beginning. As you create those systems, make sure you keep marketing and customer experience in mind. You will not remember to do those simple little things, like the interaction with Sally the cashier, unless you plan them, schedule them, and set reminders.

MARKETING CALENDAR

Speaking of scheduling, creating a marketing calendar may seem like a lot of work at first, but it is going to simplify your marketing strategies. If you spend a bit of time, perhaps an hour or two, making a schedule, that document can help immensely to keep you on track and organized in the future when it comes to marketing.

Take Action

Print the calendar from the Tool Kit in the back of the book. Print 6. Write in the MAJOR holidays that occur over the next six months, then add promotions you would like to offer. Perhaps you envision hosting a Valentine's Day card design event or offering Christmas-themed family photography mini sessions. You get the idea! Record all of this on your calendar.

Now, look at the first event and back-track four weeks. Write a reminder on your calendar to email friends, current clients, or those you think will be interested about the event or promotion. This is your first email "blast!" If you want to add them to an emailed newsletter, they *must* opt in so ask them first if it is alright to add them or have them sign up.

Following the first email blast and the actual event, consider following up with postcards to partners and vendors, postcards to clients, related blog posts, social media updates, and phone calls. Think about when these would be the most effective, or which ones would suit your business best, and get them on the calendar.

Scheduling them now will help you stay on track when the event nears and things get hectic.

Now, do the same for all the other events and promotions that you marked on your calendars! You have a marketing calendar. You can hang this where you complete most of your work, or share it with employees if you have any!

A tip that I have learned over time, is to keep your calendar after that month passes. That way, you can use it next year, see what went well, and adjust as needed.

MYTH BUSTED

Print ads are the way to go!

Seeing your name in print is fun, and I cannot deny that. It gives you a feeling of legitimacy and accomplishment. However your fiscal ledger may not balance out if you pursue this avenue in the very Beginning. Unless you are running a coupon in a local magazine (at a fair trade or price to a target demographic), try to stay away from print ads during your startup, no matter how perfect they may seem.

AMBASSADORS

It may be hard to toot your own whistle, so consider letting someone else do it for you! Instead of calling them tooters, for the purpose of this section I will refer to them as ambassadors. An ambassador is someone that has experienced your brand and your business and liked it. This person may already refer friends, comment on your social media posts, and encourage future clients. You may only know them as an acquaintance, or they may be one of your best friends; all scenarios are fine. You will want to get them on Team <u>your business name here</u>.

To start the process of bringing some ambassadors in as part of your marketing strategy (and for general support and encouragement), ask them to meet for coffee or lunch. This can seem scary, but you may be surprised at how easy it is and how open and willing they are to talk. As you meet with your first, second, or third ambassador, remind them, and yourself for that matter, that this is a business move. You are not asking them to do anything they do not want to do. Ambassadors promote, organically and naturally, your business for you, because they have experienced it and loved it.

Your goal is to provide incentive to keep them singing your praises, such as a discount on your products (large enough that they benefit, but not so large that you lose money) or use of your service at a discounted price or on a special day. This is an opportunity for them as well as you. These ambassadors are a big part of your team so reward them accordingly.

If they agree to be Team You, then it is up to you to train them and prepare them on the right things to say. It is okay to ask that they comment on posts or present your product or service in a certain manner. Do not just send them out and *hope* that they will bring you clients. Provide them with the tools to succeed, and make sure they know what exactly they are promoting. Check in with them, thank them, and follow up.

Make sure you pay attention to natural personalities before you invite an ambassador to join your team. This is not a sales job, and they need to naturally be able to talk kindly and easily to others about things in a way that sparks interest. You know who these people are already! It also helps if they are in the same "circles" as your ideal client.

MYTHS BUSTED

I will just hand out my product or give away my services for free because then those people will want to market for me.

It can be difficult but you have to be clear, and ask them to share. You are not being rude here. This is a mutually beneficial endeavor. Preface the reward with something simple like, "I'd love to share *my cool new product* with you at no cost. However, I only ask that you share it with your friends and family, post about it on social media, and add a link back to my social media saying a few words about it. Are you okay with that?" Set the expectation and do not expect more. Once the task is completed, *thank* them. You also have to have a point in which you will stop being free. Make a goal or benchmark for yourself. "Once I've profited X amount, then I'll stop giving my products/services away, even if that's tough and what some have come to expect."

Marketing is out of my price range. I will just let my friends and family promote me.

If you have set up an ambassador program, or discussed this with friends and family, then that is a great idea. But as great and wonderful as you are, without a plan or strategy in place, you will always just be the friend on Etsy, the person who probably has a website, or the free photographer. Sorry, but none of that is going to drum up business. Your family and friends love you, but you will always be their sister, daughter, friend, or spouse first. Step outside the realm of friends and family, and present potential team members with a clearly defined benefit and expectation.

SOCIAL MEDIA MARKETING

Social Media promotion is one of the best tools you have in your arsenal. Use it wisely. Blogging can bring your business to the top of Google search pages if done correctly and it only costs you some time and organization.

When promoting your business through a social media platform, "tagging" can help grow your audience organically. For instance, you sell a product on Etsy. When you email the thank you, ask if you can follow them on Facebook or Instagram. If this occurs, post a picture of the product, tag the client, and give them a sweet thank you and shout out for purchasing from you. You have now created a positive experience for your client, and also reached their audience.

This method may seem simple, but if your customer has 183 followers, chances are at least 10 saw your image and name. If your customer liked your shop, it is likely that her friends have similar tastes and interests. You may not get a sale from that post, but you are building awareness and reaching new potential clients with focused marketing. This works across multiple social media platforms.

You could take it one step further instead, and write a blog post about the sweet customer that purchased your sign and how that made you feel, changed your day, and put you in a better mood in your personal life as well. Share a positive story about the transaction. Consider linking your blog post to another social media page. It may be fun for a customer to find out that just by making a simple purchase, they altered someone else's day for the better.

You are creating a good, joyful, and valuable experience for others. Perhaps you send a handwritten card a few weeks after a purchase, an honest thank you for doing business with you. You may even make this part of your systems, so that you remember to do this with every client. These personal touches will soon start to snowball and gain traction, making clients realize that doing business with you is a pleasure!

BLOGGING

What in the world are you supposed to blog about and how do you get anyone to read it? Blogging puts you out there in a much more personal and vulnerable manner. As mentioned before, make sure to plan your blog posts in your marketing calendar. Blogs need to be consistent to keep people coming back or reading more. When you write, tie your business in with a personal aspect of your life to build a deeper relationship with your customer base.

I recently changed a wall in my office. I went to a local craft store and bought what I needed, then I posted on Instagram and wrote a short blog post. I made sure to leave a little suspense. The next post was the before and after shots, all done through the convenience of my smartphone. I added a bit of adventure to a normal everyday experience!

Plug In

As you are working on your blog, download or add a simple SEO plugin to the back end of your site. This will help optimize your search engine ranking and give you a little formula or structure for your posts.

Be Consistent

Keeping your writing style, post length, and posts per week consistent will help grow your blog. Start by scheduling a post one day a week. Add some fun content with substance, so that search engines will pick it up and place it in a results list. Keep this up and you should start climbing the ranks. However, if you are not going to blog regularly then do not blog at all. Dramatic? I do not think so; a blog should keep people coming back, and to do that, you must actually be posting.

If you have potential clients checking in on your blog every once in a while and they see the same old post, they are going to assume you are not doing anything new. While that is not true, on what else fo they have to base their opinion?

Create a Series

If you need help finding a way to post more often, consider structuring a few posts as a series, or possibly a recurring theme. This will keep readers coming back and will keep you at it!

Blog Post Ideas

Join in with the social media fun and celebrate "throwback Thursdays" or #tbt. Post about past sessions, services, or products. You can even blog about celebrations such as anniversaries or birthdays of your employees, yourself, or your clients.

Are you partnering with someone on a project, or is there a vendor event coming up? Let clients and partners alike know what you have going on. The possibilities are endless! New products, specials, new ambassadors, a DIY project at home, or tips about your skill or profession can all create great content for a blog.

COLLABORATION

As a creative business owner, you will probably be working from home, by yourself for the most part. That is why collaboration is one of my favorite aspects of being a small business owner; working together with like-minded people is great for networking, marketing, and enjoyment!

It may be easier to work on your own. You can run with your own ideas, and you are in charge. But there are definite benefits to collaborating, so go ahead, take the leap, and plan a collaborative event.

This could be a styled session, a bake off, a sidewalk art show, or anything that bring your peers together to promote your craft! The following are just a few of the benefits to a collaboration:

1. You will be meeting, collaborating, and working with fellow small business owners, growing your network and making new friends.

2. Everyone involved is gaining quality promotional material. By styling what you, the owner, want to display and showcase, you exhibit your very best in the manner you want it portrayed.

3. This is also a time to stretch your creativity. Be different; do what sets you apart with no strings attached. If you have been wanting to try something new, but no client has ever asked you to do it, now is your chance.

This truly is a time to build genuine relationships and make friends. Being asked to participate in a collaborative event will make you feel appreciated and valued. Everyone involved is doing this to showcase their craft and talents, so stay focused and organized; be your best self.

For instance, consider you are a local florist, looking to build your business. By collaborating with other local vendors to stage a styled reception shoot, complete with bride, you bring various professions together. Start asking around to find a willing photographer, dress store, model, hairdresser, makeup artist, event coordinator, party rental professional, and caterer. Set up a shoot, and the various vendors can all use the images on their social media sites, blog about the experience, tag each other, and more. You now gain access to their audiences as well, and everyone sees how you can work together to produce a stunning result!

If this is too large of an endeavor, make it even simpler. If you make necklaces, get some friends together and bring someone who is great at hair and makeup over. Have a fun girls night, getting dolled up and modelling your jewelry. Snap some photos on your smartphone and voila! Miniature collaboration! (I do suggest practicing with the phone camera and the lighting ahead of time for optimal results.)

What really makes a stunning and shareable image is the subject. Genuine laughter, fun colors, and the vibe of your brand will produce the material you want. Putting together a small or a larger scale session like this will give you great material, and friends, in this startup phase of your business. It takes some extra time and effort, but that comes along with the creative business startup territory!

What you are about to unpack in the next chapter is beneficial to polish off the startup of your business. It will tie up any loose ends and fill in any gaps left. You are going to see all these various aspects coming together and get a better idea of the direction you are headed.

Chapter Seven

Loose Ends: Tidy Up

Look how far you have come! You made it to the last chapter and you are already well on your way to setting up a small business that is going to succeed. This business will change your life and touch so many others.

DEFINING SUCCESS

Without a clear view of where you are going, how will you know you arrived? While someone much more famous and clever than I certainly said this first, it really makes so much sense. If you have not defined what success means to you and your business, then you will never consider yourself successful. If you look around and feel that your peers all look better, sound smarter, and are more successful, maybe it is time for you to really think about what success means for you.

When you are beginning anything, and especially a business, writing out goals can feel daunting or permanent. So start small. Write a goal for the day, then the week, then the month. Soon you will feel comfortable writing long term goals or thinking of the bigger picture. As you achieve the small goals, with success, you will begin to feel more confident in your ability to set and achieve larger, more complex goals. Consider the following examples.

A photographer defines success as being able to wear her pajamas to work (while editing) and having the ability to travel with her husband. The number of weddings she would like to book each year is X at $$$$ amount per wedding.

Another friend is about to open up a great little shop that sells handmade signs and decorations with messaged like **Truth and Love** scrawled across them. She defines success in her business as "creating an income from home that gets me excited to get out of bed in the morning, utilizes by strengths, serves people in need, and fulfills my desire to encourage girls and women, especially those that question their beauty and worth."

My sweet sister is not only a military wife who travels frequently, but she is also a creative designer and florist. Her definition of success is "JOSIE NEEDS TO GET THIS TO YOU ASAP."

We do not know the ins and outs of other businesses, and we do not know what their goals are, or how they define success. In any of these circumstances, it would be easy for the business owners to look at someone else, compare, and feel that they are not doing as well as they should be. However, when they take the time to define what success means to them, then they are measured on their own merits, instead of those of others.

While you and your colleagues may offer similar products or services, each is shooting for something very different, a unique goal. Therefore, you must determine your definition of success. To help you along, I will share with you a formula that I use to determine what success means in my business, and standard for meeting my own goals.

1 **Finances**

Consider the profit that you need to make from your business. Are you working in order to have a little extra spending money, to fund a yearly family vacation, to pay school tuition, or put food on the table and a roof over your head? Identify what you need to be making, in terms of a paycheck, in order to contribute to you or your family's monetary needs.

Now that you have a goal for your take home profit, determine what it will take, in terms of services and products, to reach that goal. If you need to make $5,000 a year profit, and you make an average profit of $4 on each birthday card you sell in your Etsy shop, then approximately how many cards do you need to sell each year? You need to sell about 1,250 birthday cards to bring in your desired profit. (Keep in mind, your cards may sell for $7 each, but you calculated in labor, supplies, shipping, and all the other expenses associated with the product.) You have now set your goal appropriately for your family and your business. Stop looking at what others have and do in the light of comparison.

2 **Fun**

The next part of the formula for success is to have a little fun. Identify how you want to spend your time working, what your ideal work day looks like, how many hours you will work, what your workspace should be like, and with what people you will work. Think about these details and add them to your vision.

3 **Write it Down**

Now that you have thought this out, write down your definition of success and put it in your work area. I make mine fancy by using a gold pen and displaying it in a frame. It keeps me from wallowing around when I see other photographers that book more, make more, or appear to be doing better.

A sample version of success may look like "I will sell X number of services/products in 1 year at an average price of $$ I'll be successful when I'm working _____ and spending this much time _____."

You can also write smaller goals in a similar manner. As we mentioned above, there are times when you may want to write out a goal for the day, the week, or the month.

While perhaps you use big-picture, or long term, goals to define success for your business overall, the same principles can apply to even the goal for the day or hour. However, be sure to set a time limit for your goals. "Sell more" is not a goal, but rather a vague idea. "Sell 20 more ___ by August 2017" is specific and measurable.

Your goal may change yearly. You may have another child, move cities, quit your full time job, or any other life altering experience. Your definition of success is allowed to change. The main thing is that you identify where you want to be, business-wise, at a certain point, so that you can celebrate when you achieve the goal!

4 **Other Considerations**

Social, physical, familial, financial, and intellectual factors can all be considered and included in your business goal, in your definition of success. The beauty of identifying your own personal version of what success means is that you can include aspects of life that are important to you. You can also set goals in these various areas, such as physical goals, or goals for marketing campaigns or sales.

You will also need to determine who on your team will keep you accountable. Writing something down and then sharing it with someone else *sounds* like an easy enough strategy, but actually doing it can take some motivation.

Take Action

Fill out the goals chart in the back of the book. The first column, on the left, will be a goal you would like to achieve. In the second column, write out how this applies to your life. It could be as broad as identifying a personal or business goal. It can be more specific about your business, such as a financial or productivity goal. In the third column, write out your plan to achieve this goal, the steps you need for accomplishment. Be specific!

In the final column, write your time deadline, the date by which you should accomplish this goal. You can also add one more column to the end and write down the name of your accountability partner.

FREE RESOURCES

As you begin your business startup journey, you will find that there are many resources available to you. Some aids come at a cost and can help immensely. But there are some amazing resources available out there for absolutely free that could benefit your business exponentially. You just have to be able to match their value to your business needs effectively.

The more quickly you put free into action, the more valuable it becomes. Do not become just a collector of books, courses, or programs. Before you move on to another great resource, make sure you have *fully* utilized and implemented what you need to from the previous source.

A good friend, Erin, said this about her creative startup, "I'm just picking apart all the free stuff I can get my hands on. That way, when I do get ready to spend our family money on this business startup, I know exactly what resource will benefit me the most."

Usually, one free resource tips you off to another. Potentially, you could find yourself surrounded by a wealth of information from really great people, all for the cost of time. This friend shared with me a few of the discoveries she had come across, and I looked into them. Jackpot! A few of the podcasts she sent me have changed the way I do business and even inspired parts of this book.

There are many places to find usable resources that may seem unexpected. Podcasts are available in a variety of topics, for free or very little. I found EntreLeadership to be a useful podcast when I was starting up my business.

Give away your email! Many resources are available at the cost of allowing access to your email address. Free e-books and checklists may come in handy at this small cost. Sign up for newsletters from companies that are relative to your business. Blogs of others that have been in your shoes can be helpful and encouraging as well.

Spending time sharing your ideas with others can give you new insight and makes others feel like they are part of your journey. While taking a friend out for coffee is not free, it is a lost cost for support, insight, accountability, and advice!

INNOVATION

Never give up on making your business better. Skills and strategy you have learned from this book should help ease your mind and help you gain traction from the moment those "doors" open. To keep this momentum, look to the future. Is there a new way to track your progress or better your skills, so that you remain fresh, accountable, relevant, and valuable?

Clients want to hire an innovative business that makes their experience smooth. If you are creating a product for your business, look into ways you can start to outsource or mass produce. Even looking into new ways to accept different forms of payment is being proactive and innovative in the structure of your business.

SETTING UP A REFERRAL PROGRAM

While we discussed a few marketing strategies already, a referral program may come in handy down the road. A referral program is similar to an ambassador program, but more publicized and official. You will basically reward your clients for sharing your business, as well as reward the new client that you gain from the interaction. It is an easy way to avoid being a salesperson and grow your business through encouraged word of mouth.

When asking for referrals, you are planting the seed in the client's mind to share their experience. Let them know that if they had a great experience, the best compliment they can give is a referral to their friends and people with whom they come in contact.

Offer to share with them something special for sending new clients your way. By the way, the special something needs to be pretty amazing, as they did just get you a new client. Your new client also needs to feel special and valued, so reward them as well for taking their friend's advice There are ways to get much more specific on a referral program, but you can look into that further down the road Not enough businesses offer referral incentives. If you do it right, your marketing campaign could pretty much run without you!

For example, you offer guitar lessons to kids after school. Four lessons cost $150. A referral program could offer not just one, but TWO, additional lessons when a referred friends signs up. The new student will also receive free two lessons. Similarly, you could offer a "half off" incentive of the next session for both the referrer and the referred. The referral program revolves around the idea that the new client will enjoy your services and continue to use them in the future. The referral brings them in the door. You have to keep them coming back.

KNOWING WHEN TO JOIN

Many creatives have found organizations for their skill set. An association or forum that caters directly to you and your business is out there and waiting for you. As some of these groups can cost quite a bit, knowing when to join up can be a difficult decision. Joining an organization potentially offers credibility, access to others in your line of work, and live chat sessions with "the best," and more. Before you make the leap, be sure this organization is relevant and beneficial. Many of your clients may not even know what the "Association of World Class Crafters" even is, so how would joining bring you more customers and would joining make you feel more legitimate?

Wait until you are ready to join up with an organization, so that it will grow your business not be a drain on your limited time and cash flow.

LOVE, HATE, UP, DOWN

Recently, I heard Darren Hardy, an author, speaker, and magazine publisher relate personal business to a roller coaster ride. Have you ever stood in line for a roller coaster? You are probably listening to the screams and getting excited. You jump on, snap the seat belt, and start the ascent. Up, up, up you go. Your suspense builds as you climb, along with your heart rate. Then.....BOOM! You drop, perhaps rise up out of your seat, and your heart feels like it is in your throat. Is this joy or pure terror? What turn is coming next? Will I be flipped, looped, or swung? How many more drops are there?

Running a small business is actually quite similar. You have stood in line, seen others do it, and built the excitement. You are finally in the seat and buckling up. You have no real clue what is coming next or how you are going to feel about it. Sometimes you will laugh; other times you will cry. It is going to be one of those love-hate relationships. You will find yourself up one second and at the bottom of a wild ride the next.

So how do you get through it all? First, you do not get on the ride alone. You may be in the front seat, but make sure all the other seats are full. Have someone next to you that is going to reach over and smooth your wind-blown hair back down and tell you to hold on because here comes another drop. Do not be afraid to enlist friends, family, or even other business owners to keep you accountable. Finding accountability partners and becoming part of a community is critical at this stage in your startup. Otherwise the first dip or flip that comes your way and knocks you off your feet (it will happen) may be enough to throw you off course without a friend. The drive you have to set your own hours, make more money, or be your own boss, are not enough without support.

TIME MANAGEMENT

"And once you live a good story, you get a taste for a kind of meaning in life, and you can't go back to being normal; you can't go back to meaningless scenes stitched together by the forgettable thread of wasted time," says Donald Miller.

There are going to be dozens of tips, tricks, hacks, and ideas for managing your time and becoming more productive. Part of working for yourself is being able to master, yes MASTER, your time management. Everyone is always looking for more time, and has been for centuries. Nobody ever finds it. The trick is...to make more time, so stop looking.

Email, social media, smartphones, small details, and procrastination can all result in distraction and a waste of valuable time. While answering emails is important, it can easily end up being two hours later and you did not achieve much during that time. The following are the personal ways in which I try to hone in on being productive and avoid common distractions.

Brain Dump

Emptying your brain every morning may seem like a silly task, but it is something like this that takes a few minutes of your life and can help you free up hours. It is important to start each day with a fresh perspective. Getting up 3 minutes early to complete a simple routine is worth it; I am talking 180 seconds here.

With pencil and paper in hand, set your timer for 3 minutes and dump. Write down all of the things floating around in your head. What you need to do today, what is important, what you just had to remember... just write it all down without any order or structure.

That is it; you are done. It seems simple! After this exercise, you may need to throw it away. Perhaps this is a tool you can use to elaborate and make a list or set goals. No matter if you ever use the list or not, you will feel much better getting it all out! If you have a racing mind at night, and are losing out on sleep, this may be a useful exercise at the end of the day as well.

Tick Tick

I used to be a teacher and the whole day was managed by the timer. If not, I would be waiting two hours on the same kid every day to finish a simple task. I would announce, "Four minutes on the clock! Finish your thoughts and get ready to pass your paper in."

When I resigned to start my creative business, that little timer was one of the few things I kept from my room (aside from books of course, my attic is filled with those). I now put my phone away and use a timer to control certain tasks. Setting a time limit for emails, brain dumps, and even lunch is a way to structure your time and stay focused. As a new mother, my schedule now revolves around nap times, and planning for these times has actually made me more productive. Who knew?

I also plan for a timed session of cleaning my desk (physical and on the computer). Having a clean and organized work space will make you feel organized, keep your day flowing, allow you to find the things you need, and encourages you to settle in and get work done.

Plan it Out

Plan out your whole work week, scheduling your activities in 30 minute increments. Who knows? You may even find this so effective that you start it for your personal life as well!

A blank template in the Tool Kit can be printed off and used over and over again. On the left, write your time increments. Write down all that you need to do and the time you are allotting yourself to get it completed. If you stick to this schedule, and find that some activities are completed in less time, and others are not getting done, then you can rethink where you need to focus more time.

WHAT IS NEXT?

This book has covered a wide range of topics, from setting up your website and legalities, to choosing an accounting avenue. You honed in on your brand, treating it as an experience, and received some amazing direction for marketing strategies to avoid feeling overwhelmed.

So what is next? Now what? Where do you go from here? Keep reading to find additional checklists and charts that I have prepared for your use.

Eventually you may consider some continued education, tailored specifically for your personal or business growth. The world is growing, and business is growing right along with it. Technology and new ideas are evolving overnight. Forming community and having guidance as your business starts to take off is worth investing in.

I wish you success in your new creative business startup!

The Author

My husband once found me crying in my closet. It was not my finest hour.

Running your own business is no joke. You put yourself out there, make decisions that may or may not gain momentum, and stand alone asking the world to choose you. It can feel lonely, as most of those around you do not really understand what you are going through.

Take a deep breath and relax. I have been exactly where you are standing, and I know how you feel. Trust me; I can stand with you.

I am Jen Brazeal, the woman behind Creative Business Startup, and I am deeply passionate about helping women get through the beginning stages and build a thriving, self-sufficient, and profitable business.

I taught school for over five years, and during two of those years, I started a small business from home. My photography business soon became my passion, and I decided to pursue it full time.

I soon realized that I also had a strong passion for teaching business, combining both of the things I love to do. I enjoy teaching and encouraging business owners like yourself to find success in your endeavours.

Through my book, Creative Business Startup, study guide, and CBS E-Course I am able to help women like you learn what it takes to start and sustain a successful small business. These are the tools I wish I had when I began.

To learn more about the opportunities beyond this book, visit **www.creativebusinessstartup.com**

Stay Amazing, Jen Brazeal